P9-EAJ-874

WITHDRAWN

Learning to Read, Step by Step!

Ready to Read   Preschool–Kindergarten
• big type and easy words • rhyme and rhythm • picture clues
For children who know the alphabet and are eager to begin reading.

Reading with Help   Preschool–Grade 1
• basic vocabulary • short sentences • simple stories
For children who recognize familiar words and sound out new words with help.

Reading on Your Own   Grades 1–3
• engaging characters • easy-to-follow plots • popular topics
For children who are ready to read on their own.

Reading Paragraphs   Grades 2–3
• challenging vocabulary • short paragraphs • exciting stories
For newly independent readers who read simple sentences with confidence.

Ready for Chapters   Grades 2–4
• chapters • longer paragraphs • full-color art
For children who want to take the plunge into chapter books but still like colorful pictures.

STEP INTO READING® is designed to give every child a successful reading experience. The grade levels are only guides; children will progress through the steps at their own speed, developing confidence in their reading. The F&P Text Level on the back cover serves as another tool to help you choose the right book for your child.

Remember, a lifetime love of reading starts with a single step!

Text copyright © 1989 by Natalie Standiford.
Illustrations copyright © 1989 by Donald Cook.
Cover illustration copyright © 2014 by Tim Jessell
All rights reserved. Published in the United States by Random House Children's Books, a division
of Random House LLC, a Penguin Random House Company, New York.
Step into Reading, Random House, and the Random House colophon are registered trademarks of
Random House LLC.
Visit us on the Web!
StepIntoReading.com
randomhouse.com/kids
Educators and librarians, for a variety of teaching tools, visit us at
RHTeachersLibrarians.com
Library of Congress Cataloging-in-Publication Data
Standiford, Natalie.
The bravest dog ever : the true story of Balto / by Natalie Standiford ;
illustrated by Donald Cook. p. cm. — (Step into reading. A step 3 book)
Summary: Recounts the life of Balto, the sled dog who braved a snowstorm
to deliver medicine to Nome, Alaska, during a 1925 diphtheria epidemic.
ISBN 978-0-394-89695-3 (pbk.) — ISBN 978-0-375-97416-8 (lib. bdg.)
1. Balto (Dog.)—Juvenile literature.
2. Sled dogs—Alaska—Nome—Biography—Juvenile literature.
3. Diphtheria—Alaska—Nome—Prevention—Juvenile literature.
[1. Balto (Dog) 2. Sled dogs. 3. Dogs. 4. Diphtheria—Alaska—Nome.
5. Alaska—History—1867–1959.]
I. Cook, Donald, ill. II. Title. III. Series: Step into reading. Step 3 book.
SF428.7 .S7 2003 636.73—dc21 2002013216
Printed in the United States of America
85 84 83
This book has been officially leveled by using the F&P Text Level Gradient™ Leveling System.
Random House Children's Books supports the First Amendment and celebrates the right to read.

The Bravest Dog Ever
The True Story of
BALTO

by Natalie Standiford
illustrated by Donald Cook

Random House 🏠 New York

This is a true story

about a very brave dog.

His name was Balto.

The year was 1925.

Balto lived in Nome, Alaska.

Nome was a frontier town.

Most of the year it was buried

under ice and snow.

In winter there was no way

to travel through all that ice and snow.

Not on planes or trains or boats or cars.

The only way to travel in Alaska

was by dog sled.

Balto was a sled dog.

He worked for a gold-mining company

not far from Nome.

He helped carry food and tools

to the miners.

It was a good life for a sled dog.

Balto's driver was named Gunnar.

Gunnar made Balto his lead dog.

The lead dog runs in front

of the team.

He follows the trail.

All the other dogs do

whatever the lead dog does.

So the lead dog has to be

the smartest and strongest dog of all.

One cold winter day

a terrible thing happened in Nome.

Two children got very sick.

Their parents called the doctor.

He was the only doctor

in the whole town.

When the doctor saw the children

he was very worried.

The children had a terrible sickness.

It was called diphtheria (dif-THEER-ee-ah).

The doctor did not have

the medicine he needed.

Without the medicine

the children would die.

Without the medicine

many other people in Nome

would get diphtheria and die too.

The doctor knew

he had to get some medicine—fast.

The hospital in Anchorage, Alaska,

had the medicine.

But Anchorage was 800 miles away.

The doctors in Anchorage

put the medicine on a train.

But soon the train got stuck

in the deep snow.

The train was still 700 miles

from Nome!

The people of Nome held a meeting.

Everyone was very scared.

"What are we going to do?"

asked the doctor.

"We have to get that medicine."

At last someone said,

"What about a dog-sled relay?

When one team of dogs gets tired,

a new team will be ready to take over."

The room buzzed with excitement.

That did seem like the quickest way

to get the medicine.

But the doctor frowned.

"It will still take about fifteen days.

That's a long time. Too long."

Maybe the doctor was right.

But there was no other choice.

So the mayor spoke over the radio.

"Please help!" he said.

"We need the best drivers and dogs

to help save our town!"

Gunnar heard the mayor on the radio.

Gunnar knew he had the best dog team

and the best lead dog.

Balto would come to the rescue.

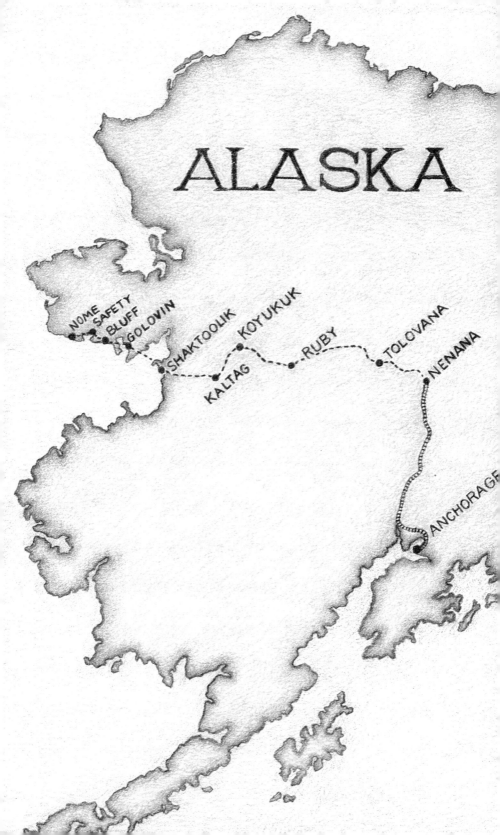

On January 27, 1925,

the race to Nome began.

Twenty-one dog teams

were in the relay.

Each team waited at a different stop.

The first driver took the medicine
from the train.
He wrapped it in fur
to keep it from freezing.
Then he drove his dogs
as fast as he could to the second stop.
He made his run in good time.

But soon the wind began to blow hard.

The air grew colder.

A blizzard was coming!

It was one of the worst storms ever.

Still the race went on.

Somehow each dog team made it

to the next stop.

In one team, two dogs froze to death.

So the driver hitched himself

to the sled.

He helped the rest of his dogs

pull through the storm.

Gunnar and Balto waited
at their stop in Bluff.
They were going to run 31 miles
from Bluff to Point Safety.
That was the second-to-last part
of the race.
But the storm had slowed things down.
Gunnar had been waiting for two days.
He did not sleep.
He wanted to be ready to go
as soon as the medicine arrived.

At last Gunnar heard dogs barking.

The medicine was here!

He put it on the sled

with a small stove and a little food.

Then he hitched up his dogs.

Balto stood proudly in the lead.

Gunnar cracked his whip.

"Mush!" he cried.

That meant "go."

The team ran out into the snowy night.

At first the team made good time.

But soon snowdrifts blocked the trail.

The dogs sank up to their necks

in snow.

They could not move.

Some began to panic.

But not Balto.

He stayed calm.

That helped the other dogs

while Gunnar dug them out

of the snow.

At last the team was on its way again.

Then the team crossed a frozen river.

The dogs and the sled

slipped and skidded on the ice.

Oh, no! Over went the sled.

Gunnar got it up again.

But the medicine was gone!

Wildly Gunnar dug for the medicine.

He could not see

through the heavy snow.

But at last he felt the package.

He put it back on the sled.

The team kept going

across the river.

Suddenly Balto stopped short.

"Mush, Balto!" shouted Gunnar.

But Balto did not move.

Then Gunnar saw why.

The ice was cracking!

If the team fell into the river,

they would all drown.

Balto had stopped just in time.

"Smart dog!" Gunnar told him.

Then he saw that Balto's feet were wet.

If they froze,

Balto would never walk again.

Quickly Gunnar unhitched Balto

from the sled.

He led the dog
to a patch of powdery snow.
Gunnar rubbed Balto's paws
in the powder.
Soon they were dry.
Balto was ready to go once more.

Balto led the team

around the cracking ice.

At last they reached

solid land again.

Were they still on the trail?

Gunnar had no idea.

The snow blew so hard,

Gunnar could not see

his own hands.

But Balto had run this trail

many times before.

Now it was all up to him.

Finally the storm died down.

Gunnar saw Point Safety just ahead.

"Balto did it!" thought Gunnar.

He couldn't wait to warm his hands
by a cozy fire.

But all the lights were out
at Point Safety.

Was the next driver there?

Gunnar did not know.

And there was no time to find out.

So Gunnar and Balto did not stop.

They had never been so tired.

But they raced on through the night
toward Nome.

It was just before dawn.

The sky began to glow.

In the town of Nome

everyone was sleeping.

Gunnar and his team pulled into town.

They had made it!

Balto was too tired to bark.

They had been on the trail

for 20 hours straight.

They had driven 53 miles!

Gunnar took the medicine to the doctor.

The doctor was surprised.

He thought it would take 15 days

to get the medicine.

But Gunnar delivered it

after only five and a half days!

"Thank you, Gunnar!" said the doctor.

"You are a hero!"

"Balto is the hero," said Gunnar.

"I could not have done it without him."

The doctor went right to work.

He gave the medicine

to all the sick people.

In a few days they would be well.

The town of Nome was saved.

All over America

people cheered for Balto.

They read about his bravery

in the newspaper.

Balto was the most famous dog

in the world.

A year later

the people of New York City

put up a statue of Balto.

It still stands in Central Park.

Lots of children play on the statue.

They remember Balto,

the bravest dog ever!

31901060652452